TRIUMPH HOUSE
Poetry with a Purpose

A Tapestry Of Love

Edited by

CHRIS WALTON

First published in Great Britain in 1999 by
TRIUMPH HOUSE
1-2 Wainman Road, Woodston,
Peterborough, PE2 7BU
Telephone (01733) 230749

All Rights Reserved

Copyright Contributors 1998

HB ISBN 1 86161 413 6
SB ISBN 1 86161 418 7

Foreword

We all feel affection towards something or someone within our lives. *A Tapestry Of Love* joins new and established poets sharing with us personal and in some cases religious thoughts and experiences about love, friendship and admiration.

There is no more appropriate form of expression to use than poetry. Over the years poetry has become an extremely popular form of communication. We believe you will find *A Tapestry Of Love* inspiring and thought provoking.

This collection will become a family favourite among the poet and poetry lover for years to come.

Chris Walton
Editor

CONTENTS

A Silhouette	Grace Wade	1
An Enigma	Harold E Pearce	2
The Banner Of Life	Ray Varley	4
Take My Heart	Margaret Howens	5
The Happening	Olive Iris Smith	6
Aloneness	R Stoker	7
Life	Charlene Bishop	8
Belief	Theresa Hartley	9
Conquering Love	Cicily E Long	10
My Love Across The Atlantic	Ann Forshaw	11
When All Seems Lost	Heather Y V Henning	12
Swallows' Delight	Heather Kirkpatrick	13
Immortality	David J Burke	14
John The Baptist	Carolyn Long	15
Oh Jesus	Betty Crookes	16
The Valley	Ethel Elizabeth Deeks	17
Patient Thoughts	Wendy Watkins	18
Let Us Live But One Day At A Time	William Price	19
In Brevity, Lies Truth	T Burke	20
Jesus In The Snow	Paul Gainsford Bailey	21
Life In The Twentieth Century	Judy Studd	22
Freedom	G J Hutchings	23
Forever Yours	Margaret Jackson	24
The Lighthouse	G Cripwell	25
My Reason For Living	Linda Roberts	26
Happiness Is A Homeland	S Chesterman	28
Never Again	Kenneth Anthony McCormack	29
Pain Of An Angel	Carol Lewis	30
Ninian, Holy Light	Bill Hayles	31
Prayer	Graham Kirman	32
The Artist And The Picture	J Lomas	33
Nature God	Jean Paisley	34
Channels Of Peace	Pat Melbourn	35
El Niño	Joyce Newlin	36
Pictures From The Nativity	Sheila Burnett	37

The Cross	Joe De La Mare	38
Your Will	Jay	39
On Turning A Blind Eye	Eunice Harding	40
The Spur Of Liberty	Brandan Friel	42
Jesus, My Saviour	Jessica Bomford	43
Out Of Darkness Into Light	Edith Ditchburn	44
Comfort In Bereavement	E Brace	45
Death And Rebirth	Tony Cashmore	46
Hear This My People Israel	Chris Esom	48
O Dove Of Peace	Christopher P Gillham	50
Untitled	A C Edwards	51
How To Cope With The Problems In Life	Robert Doherty	52
My Master's Voice	Stephanie Berry	53
Omagh	Frank Scott	54
The Explorer	David Overland	55
Buzzing	Mandy Roberts	56
Calvary	Max Gray	57
The Hind Of The Morning	T C Adams	58
Silent Prayer	Kathy Stewart	60
The Gift Of Life	Andrew Lawler	61
The Feast	Betty Jones	62
A Troubled Friend	Anne McLeod	63
For My Parents And My Children	Phil Millichip	64
The Night Our Hope Was Born	Alwyn Wilson	65
Untitled	Isobel Howden	66
At A Winter Dawn	John Barnes	67
Hands	Sue Fenton	68
Pilgrimage	Judith A Pye	69
Open Verdict	Vera Boyle	70
Spring (or Resurrection)	Jean Wilford Hodgson	71
Insects	Irene Tester	72
Holy Innocents' Day	Derek N Thorp	73
St Olaf's Wasdale Head	Monica Ditmas	74
Was It For Me, Lord?	Stella Morton	75
Christmas Day	Derek Marshall	76
Sorrow	Emrys George	77

Reassurance	Eileen M Pratt	78
Before You Get Angry	E Gwen Gardner	79
Friends' Meeting	Walter Birmingham	80
Our Lady's Statue	Penny Fenn Clark	81
The Poet Momentarily Sees His Surroundings Transformed	R E Hope-Simpson	82
Hold Me	Charlie Blackfield	84
The Morrow's Dawn	D J Cleeves Snr	85
Murder At The Damascus Gate	Tony Latham	86
Why?	Shirley Cowling	88
Are You A Christian?	David Senior	89
The Bible	Mary Skelton	90
Seeds	Elizabeth Rumsey	91
The Face Of Christ	Winnie Oakley	92
Snapshots	Wendy Mead	93
Who Needs A Telephone?	Euphemia McKillop	94
A Future	Vernon Breese	95
Love	Elizabeth Lang	96
He Has Risen	Janet Cavill	97
What Is Wrong?	Joe Latham	98
Parsifal: Or Good Friday Falls On All Fools' Day	Peter Mullen	99
A New Life	Norma M Smith	100
A Note Without A Song	Louie Horne	101
My Lord	Meryl Tookaram	102
A Christmas Poem	Beryl Johnson	103
Street Song	Ramsay Hall	104
Sings Of The Kingdom Of God	Gill Sathyamoorthy	105
Snake In A Tree	Andrew Moll	106
Martyrdom	Teresa Finlayson	107
Jerusalem	Patrick Barker	108
Love And Faith	Albert King	109
Untitled	M Petch	110

A Silhouette

A word for enchantment, a silhouette,
Conjures up moonlight, dreamworld, shadows, shy coquette,
A camel still on moon-drenched strand,
Proud head held high, hooves in sand,
A burnous clad figure by his side,
Zephyr-like whisper around him glide.

A hillside shadowed as day turns to dusk,
Birds, animals, silhouette as onward they thrust,
Their journey not knowing to any but they,
Just their own 'over the hill and far, far away',
A presence left on sky and heather,
Silhouettes by moonlight, camaraderie together.

Grace Wade

AN ENIGMA

There is much we do not understand,
Especially suffering, in God's Plan;
We only know it has its roots
Way back, in the fall of Man.

At Creation all God did was good,
Man was the crowning glory of it all,
Then Satan came upon the scene,
His cunning engineered the fall of Man.

Man's perfection flawed
Destroyed perfection throughout all creation,
Sin spread its deadly cancer
Through every tribe and nation.

Violence, sickness, death,
Became a part of life,
The peace that Earth once knew
Replaced by greed and strife.

The realm of nature too
Saw drastic change take place,
Its original perfection
We can no longer trace.

Human nature, flawed by sin,
Lost the health it once enjoyed,
Our inbuilt sinful nature
Perfect health destroyed.

Suffering often gives no warning,
No time to prepare,
One day we are well and happy,
Then suddenly, the trouble's there.

It comes in many forms,
To rich and poor alike,
It is not possible to know
Who next it will strike.

When trouble comes to me
My faith gives strength to cope,
It makes the heartache bearable,
As I live in faith and hope.

Harold E Pearce

THE BANNER OF LIFE

The banner of life, is a banner of grace,
A banner of love, a life to embrace.
'Tis a banner of sharing, and caring for others,
A banner of friendship, with sisters and brothers.
The banner of life, is a banner of peace,
A banner of kindness,
Where forgiveness, does not cease.
The banner of life, is compassion for the needy,
A banner of unselfishness,
A banner that's not greedy.
The banner of life, is falling now and then,
'Tis a banner of strength
That lifts you up once again.
The banner of life, does not slander or hate,
But communicates love
As words leave the gate.
The banner of life, is a banner of songs,
When joy stirs the heart,
When love covers all wrongs.
The banner of life is walking upright,
Rejoicing in truth,
And doing what's right.
The banner of life is a banner of hope,
A banner of mercy,
When we need grace to cope.
The banner of life when flying at full-mast,
Looks to a brighter, better future,
To a life that will last.
The banner of life, that breathed life into me,
Was the banner of love,
That hung on the tree.

     Amen.

Ray Varley

TAKE MY HEART

Take my heart it belongs to you
Ne'er no other one will do
'Cause my love shall ever be
Only yours for all eternity
Come because I offer you
My loving heart that shall e'er be true
O' sweetheart take my heart
Pray let it be for some part
To give your love in return
Take my heart to ease the pain
For always time and time again
Such a burning desire to hold you
'Cause my love for you is true
Yet here's hoping you shall return
Sweet emotion to e'er burn
With equal loving desire to entwine
Thine heart ever with mine
If only your eyes could see
How deep the love is in my heart for thee
So take my heart it belongs to you
Because I offer a love so true
Oh! Take my heart.

Margaret Howens

THE HAPPENING

Could I have known before this day was done,
That fate's dark clouds would so blot out the sun
And leave me in the world alone
A prayer to loneliness and fear
My heart lies like the frozen bough
Cold still, for it is winter now
If I must walk in Hager's way
A wilderness so dark and drear
Then walk with me, pray walk with me
I long to feel your presence near
And I will lift my tear-stained face
And lean on you, oh, God of Grace
And in the future's timeless way
Your balm upon my heart will lay.

Olive Iris Smith

ALONENESS

Coming to it, some
Seeking it, others
Running from it, many
Its reflected glory and glare
No-one avoids.
Talking of it we learn and
Recognise its power. To
Comprehend it we can't we don't,
Running from it we are encompassed;
Sooner than later its
Steel-pinned nailed-fingers
Encase and enclose the runner
Pinioning and mounting him
To the board of life.
In seeking it, the lingerer soon
Tires of its rhythmic glare, and
Time tolls a heavier beat.
To be with us always like our
Own mouth's sap
Running at first a thin
Birth-mist then drowning us
Finally in its fog-green tentacles.

R Stoker

LIFE

The baby in the pram with no concern in life;
He being so sweet, so innocent, he doesn't get into strife.
He lays so vulnerable, caressed with protection;
From life, harm and worry he has no subjection!

He feeds without having the need to hunt;
He sleeps peacefully, no danger to confront.
He feels warmth and comfort, so very secure;
If only this life could forever endure!

As one ages, the wider the world opens to them;
The mould begins to set, the seeds transform to stem.
The child becomes an adult with many dangers to confront;
For his food, comfort and security, he has no choice but to hunt!

The world sees you face to face;
One has to live at a steady pace.
If you fall back, expect no concern;
The world is so cruel, so evil so stern!

Charlene Bishop

BELIEF

Believing in something or someone
Helps quite a lot
Gives one strength that others have not
Gives one hope to help one cope
Believing is a beautiful thing
Especially believing in God our King!

Theresa Hartley

CONQUERING LOVE

Like a mighty warrior
He strides out
across the earth
in vulnerability
to conquer
by dying
glorious
humble
wearing a crown of thorns
His robe
blood-red
His feet
nail-pierced
shod with peace
His hands
wounded,
hold His sceptre
His Cross
His name is Love.

He will capture
for freedom
He will open your eyes
to glory
open your heart
to love
open your life
to live

O' surrender
surrender
To Him
whose name is
Love.

Cicily E Long

MY LOVE ACROSS THE ATLANTIC

I wish I was a magician
Who could perform special magic today;
To bring our shores much closer
So I could see you every day.
For being the miles apart we are
I long so much to see you;
So we can share the love we have
And make our dreams come true.

But as I am no magician
I shall pray to God instead;
That the times we share together
Are not too far ahead.
With each and every passing day
The waiting gets harder you see;
As I'm sure you know this already my love
But you are so special to me.

Oh how I wish I was a magician
And could magic your shores my way;
For then I would not be sitting here
Writing this today.
But until the happy time arrives
When we are not apart;
I sit at home and wait for you
With a sad and aching heart.

Ann Forshaw

WHEN ALL SEEMS LOST

When all seems lost and hope is gone,
Cheer up and smile and carry on.
When trouble seems to have no end,
Have faith and you will find a friend.

If people seem unkind to you,
Be patient, you will find it's true:
The Lord is with you every day.
Just trust and He will show the way.

Heather Y V Henning

SWALLOWS' DELIGHT
(In memory of Rupert a likeable rogue)

The swallows flew on their first sortie of the day
They dive-bombed Rupert relentlessly
Rupert sauntered down the yard, ignoring their bravery.
He was not intimidated by anyone or anything
Rupert was king.

The boss of all the cats on the farm, Rupert held little charm
With many notches to his belt, he knew how to make his
                                                     presence felt.
Even the chocolate teapot was afraid of him, and she was
                                            next in line to the throne.
For Rupert was the fiercest cat that she had ever known.

One day while crossing the road, he forgot to use the Highway Code!
The swallows did loops in the sky, they performed a trapeze in
                                              the barn that night.
Rupert the king was dead, and they could not conceal their delight.

The chocolate teapot lay by the fire, she began to preen.
So she purred, the king is dead.
Long live the queen.

Heather Kirkpatrick

IMMORTALITY

No mortal soul has ever seen
Through the eyes of Heaven above
Never witnessed such wonderments
The beauty of these visions of love.
In the momentary passing of body to spirit
As the halls of darkness fill with light
Pictures of Heaven are seen by those
Granted safe passage and eternal sight.

David J Burke

JOHN THE BAPTIST

Before John did his earthly work
He purged himself of sin
He lived on locusts and wild honey
Until he was worthy to begin,
To pave the way for Jesus Christ
The one true Son of God
And in the shallows of Jordan River,
Gave two for the price of one -
He spoke about 'The Coming' at length,
And washed away their sins
He warned all men of the wrath of God
That the kingdom was close at hand
The Baptist sent to man by God
To turn the world's hard heart
Before he saw the sweetest lamb
Who took away their sins,
And showered water, and Holy Ghost
Upon His Holy Head.
With God's grace shining through His eyes
He knew His work was done
He'd done what He'd been sent to do
The rest earned extra points.

Carolyn Long

OH JESUS

Oh Jesus it's good to know you are there
Especially when no-one seems to care
When family fall out and it ends with a row
Oh Jesus I need your love right now.

Oh Jesus it's good to know you are close
When the work is not shared, 'cos I do the most
When I'm tired - weary - fed-up with life
Oh Jesus it's great that you'll take all my strife

Oh Jesus it's good to know you're my friend
When things that happen send me round the bend
When everything seems to be in a mess
Oh Jesus I'm glad that in you I can rest

Oh Jesus it's good to know that you're near
When life causes me to shed more than one tear
When it comes to a point that I must make a stand
Oh Jesus, thank you that I can hold on to your hand

Oh Jesus it's good to know that you only
Will take care of me when I'm sad and lonely
When I'm aching and hurting and filled with such pain
Oh Jesus it's wonderful to just call your name

Oh Jesus it's good to know that you care for me
That you suffered and died that I might be free
That you know my name and all of my ways
And will always be with me, till the end of my days.

Betty Crookes

THE VALLEY

My load seemed heavy
More than I could bear:
Each day I seemed more weary
I turned to Jesus in my despair.
He took my hand and led me
To see that in the valley there,
Trees and plants were growing
And flowers were everywhere.
I now know that in the valley
Is where faith and love will grow;
It is where my Lord is with me
His love and grace to show.
So when I climb the mountain top
And as once again I view,
To see the wonders of God's grace
His love and mercy too,
I shall give thanks and praises
To the Father God above;
For the way that He has led me
And for all His wondrous love.

Ethel Elizabeth Deeks

PATIENT THOUGHTS

I shall not pursue the rocky path,
which is open for me to explore.
Not yet anyway - for there is no need
to tackle what fate has in store.
Why should I walk on a prickly road
be cut by the blade of a knife,
When things are alright at the moment
unfilled with battle and strife.

My thoughts are optimistic
And there is much to do.
God has sent a precious gift
for me to carry through.
Of course my heart doth dream,
Love is like a rose,
But some time in the future . . .
Love may then impose.

Yes - you may be waiting,
But wait, oh wait, you must
For I must gain an inner strength
before my heart can trust.
When the time is right,
Fate will intervene,
Then you . . . will come to me,
Like an unexpected dream.

Wendy Watkin

LET US LIVE BUT ONE DAY AT A TIME

Is there a tomorrow?
Perhaps there is, but I shall not fear it
I shall live only for today
And not be afraid of tomorrow.
I shall welcome each day with a little love
A little understanding, a little patience.
Some may say the older we get, the wiser we are,
I wonder if that is so.
Would a wise man throw away another day
Because he fears tomorrow?

William Price

IN BREVITY, LIES TRUTH

I grant you five more minutes to live; reveal departing thoughts!
What was previously important is now a fine bundle of noughts.
Life's tiny candle is faintly flickering, almost thirsting to go out.
What is the bursting urgency in your mind, rushing madly about?

To bid farewell to your dear ones and know they are by your side.
To visualise their sorrowing faces and imprint them deeply inside.
You are unable to speak but you can feel that they mourn for you.
Your weak, failing hand stretches towards them as you bid 'Adieu.'

You sense in a few moments, that eternity attempts a wild jump,
That, in a lurch of accelerated velocity, they're by you in a bump.
So what seemed lost shall soon be found as all stay by your side.
Time, is only for us earthbound creatures, a microsecond wide!

T Burke

JESUS IN THE SNOW

Jesus in the snow,
Icicle on a toe,
Our Creator warms the blood,
In the winter season.

Snow on snow,
And snow on snow,
As the winter winds blow.

Born in a stable,
Light of the world,
Jesus our Saviour,
Creator of all,
There is none braver,
In all the winter's fall.

Paul Gainsford Bailey

LIFE IN THE TWENTIETH CENTURY

With no clarity of vision I stand alone. Isolated. I am mocked by uncertainty. Doubt as a vulture hangs suspended in my mind awaiting on the death-throes of reason. The fog curls insidiously, smothering the sky and eclipsing the sun. Cobwebs of confusion surround me threatening my sanity.

And hyenas crowd around me awaiting to steal away my conviction, my hope, my peace, my love; the lifeblood of my service. Wolves howl menacingly in the dark night, hungry for my joy.

Nothing seems tangible in this ethereal wilderness.

But suddenly an eagle soared gracefully overhead, far above the trees it glided as though pursuing life itself. It swooped and found its prey on the ground and silently soared upwards, ever upwards and flew effortlessly onward. Onward to its eyrie to feed its young.

The answer was revealed. You bid me rise up, call me away, your tears soaking my heart. You make me ride on wings of eagles, far above the world whilst hyenas and wolves retreat into the forests and woodlands where they belong.

I have a choice to make. I can choose life or death, renewal or hibernation.

Judy Studd

FREEDOM

With pride, I stand at the side of selfless men
Who laid down their lives and died
With pledge, to further, defend their loved ones
And the many others, that survived.
To teach all our future generations
The folly and the strife
Of prejudice, dire terrorism
At the cost of human life.

The freedom that we all embrace today
Was fought on both land and sea
And in the air among threatening clouds
That all men on earth be freed.
We must learn to respect all nations
On this earth our God provides
And thank the brave who perished
Towards Heaven, where they reside.

G J Hutchings

FOREVER YOURS

Always and forever
a friend eternally,
Such love within our hearts
tomorrow's hope then see.

Golden rays of sunshine
rainbow's glory to share,
Uplifting, this splendour
blessings found everywhere.

Dark clouds fade then sparkle
those silver linings shine.
Grant grace for all the trials
Stillness, peace so divine.

Patience be rewarded
renew our strength each day.
Much courage and wisdom
all endless joys to stay.

Everlasting grandeur
your radiance so bright,
Gently flow your spirit
for Lord you are our light.

Margaret Jackson

The Lighthouse

There she stands, all alone,
Her bright beams shining across the foam,
Helping ships from other lands,
Safe home to port with their contrabands.
To all who sail the mighty seas, a
Pillar of strength the lighthouse is.
Sailing ships, merchant ships,
Ships of every kind - are happy to
Wave to the keeper as they sail closely by.
But when it is a foggy night
There is no beam across the foam,
So into God's keeping they sail for home.

G Cripwell

My Reason For Living

With God in my life it has changed for the better
My character has deepened and my heart has grown warmer.

I love God and give Him first place in my heart
Wanting to be close to Him, never ever to be apart.

I want to show my love for God by obeying Him
By trying to be like Him, and turning away from sin.

God offers me forgiveness in exchange for my repentance
Filling me with inner love, joy, peace and contentment.

I am totally dependent on God the One who made me
Without Him in my life it would be so empty.

My reason for living comes from having a relationship with God
He protects, guides, comforts me, my problems He takes care of.

I love God with all my heart, soul, strength and mind
Every day I make sure I give Him a lot of my time.

When I am down, depressed and not feeling well
I go to God my Father as His child, a little girl.

I frequently fail God but He still goes on loving me
My desire is to please Him and make Him happy.

I believe, have faith and trust God with my life
And whatever I do for Him is not a sacrifice.

Having God in my life every day I shall never be lonely
As He is always near and will never ever leave me.

God comes first in my life the one I want to be with
Living His way, being like Him, is the best way to live.

The purpose of my life is to glorify God forever
Serving, pleasing, obeying Him, loving like no other.

Being close to God means I share His love with others
All those around me, my family, friends, and neighbours.

God is not just for the famous, rich, or nice people
He loves everyone and wants to take care of us all.

The greatest thing in the world is to know God, Our Father
Knowing that one day we can be with Him and live forever.

Linda Roberts

HAPPINESS IS A HOMELAND

I'm going back to my childhood home
Sleepy village with green orchard groves
With fields and trees blue skies and streams
Was that really real or just rose-tinted dreams?
Nearing my village in the county of Kent
Will it be the same, what do I expect?
In these days of high-rise and highways
Will my little village be just the same?
I feel real good as I change down gears
To be back here after all these years
Pull up by the old school wall
That somehow now looks rather small
The old village green is still the same
Blissfully unaware of all the change
A walk through the woods to the farm by the fields
My fairytale village is still for real
A few familiar faces I can now see
Old Mr Black still loves Mrs Green
And this mighty oak I played in as a child
My friends and I could see for miles
Here's my old house, my childhood home
With family and friends it was a good home
Through grassy meadows, I used to walk
In those faraway days when neighbours used to talk
So many memories, so many people
The shops, the pub, the old church and its steeple
As I get back in my car and turn the key
I know my little village will always be here for me.

S Chesterman

NEVER AGAIN

When you try to forget, the hurt from
The past, it's hard to resist,
The love that you missed, what can I say?
Never again, oh, never again,
No more pain, who's to blame?

When you think of your love,
Your eyes fill with tears,
For all those loving years.
Never again, oh, never again
No more pain, who's to blame?

Is it second time around, for you and me?
Will it be the same, that magic flame?
What can I say?
Never again, oh, never again,
No more pain, who's to blame?

Kenneth Anthony McCormack

PAIN OF AN ANGEL

She raised up her head, as it started to rain,
I then saw her eyes and felt her great pain,
This small huddled figure, so tiny and frail,
Her hair long and knotted, her face drawn and pale.

Glassy and bloodshot, from rivers of tears,
Her dark sunken sockets, emitted her fears,
So sad and so desperate, for someone to care,
Somebody to notice, the child crouching there.

The children around her, continue their games,
Some of them mocking and calling her names,
Though this wasn't the reason why she was so sad,
At least they acknowledged her, that wasn't so bad!

But her anguish was deeper, so deeply intense,
For on the way home, this child's fear would commence,
Home was 'that place', this frail mite was abused,
As a whore! And a punch bag! This small child was used.

Up five concrete steps she'd climbed to her hell,
And that sinking gut feeling that she knew so well!
Crept upon her once more, like a beast of the night,
No more could she struggle, her answer was - flight!

Tearful but hopeful, she fled from 'that place'
Through the wind and the rain which thrashed at her face
Tired and hungry and soaked to her vest
The harsh icy wind commanded her - rest!

Her frozen stiff body was found the next day,
God came for His angel and took her away,
No more would she suffer, this frail tiny mite,
Now safe from harm, secure in God's light!

Carol Lewis

NINIAN, HOLY LIGHT

In the year of Our Lord, AD 398,
Ninian was trained and ordained in Rome,
then leaving by the northern gate,
this blessed saint began his journey home.

In bonny Scotland among Pictish clans,
His 'shining house' he built on a rock,
from here he told them of God's plans,
these northern men were of sturdy stock.

After his return to the Britons' land,
King Tudvael grew jealous of his fame,
and so he banished him out of hand,
But Ninian continued to heal the lame.

But God took away Tudvael's sight,
in panic he sent for his holy foe,
When Ninian heard of the king's plight
to the king's side he was bound to go.

Laying our hands, the king's sight returned,
the sovereign knew he had been so wrong,
a valuable lesson he had learned,
his faith in God, from then he was strong.

Many came to Christ through Ninian,
His churches and monasteries grew in power,
He continued to restore sight, life and limb,
and his holy light shone like a tower.

Bill Hayles

PRAYER

Prayer
Prayer is the lovely thing
Prayer to God makes my heart sing
Prayer opens the throne room to the king

Prayer by day prayer by night

Prayer utilises Holy Ghost power
For a fight in the heavenly realms
Prayer injures the devil's bite
It strips him of his weedy might

When you pray the blood of Jesus over someone's life
It cuts into the heavenlies
It dispels earthly strife
It shoots with the full force of a gun rifle
The victory over sin and death
No demons can ever stifle
Jesus won our deliverance on the Cross
So the enemy can only suffer
Endless eternal loss.

Graham Kirman

The Artist And The Picture

He painted a picture I stood by his side,
Men fighting in battle, like flowers had died.
I saw earth's strong sons, was it right, was it just
That children of mothers, lay rotting in dust?

He painted weak children, eyes staring at me,
Thin lips to me pleading, and bones I could see
Small children of mothers, was it right was it wrong
That the world hurried onwards whilst children were gone?

He painted earth's vice dens, of drugs and abuse,
Of youths blindly seeking their souls to amuse.
I wept as I looked, was it right, could it be
So few reached to save them, no hope could they see?

He painted a picture of nuclear war,
Of horror long-dreaded and none to implore.
Powers choosing for mankind, to live or to die,
So cruelly hounded, none hearing their cry.

Violent men planting bombs in their strife
Strikes and no jobs, where tempers were rife.
Children's minds bruised in a turbulent mob,
Marriages broken . . . and babes left to sob.

He painted God giving a free will to all,
Not man as a robot to stand or to fall,
But to take hold of life to seek out the good
And aim for a goal in the place where he stood.

And I saw in this picture men hold hands in prayer.
United to stand, helping those in despair.
Telling earth's people, to hear God's last call
Pleading through Christ's blood salvation for all.

J Lomas

NATURE GOD

To me God is the air we breathe moving
the trees around,
the sunshine all of nature's things that
do on Earth abound.

When walking on a country path and looking
at the birds,
you can almost touch the lilies thinking
of his words.

Remembering how the seasons swiftly bring
an autumn freeze,
nature is God-given you can feel him in the
breeze.

Even when leaves drop brown and withered
on the grass,
autumnal yellow, reds and browns draw your
sight as you pass.

So, maybe we can be less as we age and still
to him,
have just a small light glowing that we hope
shall never dim.

And then as it grows darker he may move us
to his light,
where we shall live forever full of glory
ever bright.

Jean Paisley

CHANNELS OF PEACE

We are to be channels -
So let us keep the peace
That God so gladly gives to us
When we 'let our troubles cease'.

The only way to do this
Is to hand our burdens to the Lord -
And receive the peace that comes to all
When 'serving' in accord.

If we lack this special peace
Then nothing can we do -
As channels we are useless -
So let us give God His due.

The anger that we have inside
Destroys us so completely -
And if handing problems to our God
Is, in a way, defeatist.

Our Saviour, Jesus, comes to us -
A willing media-tor -
Who listens to our every word -
The Son of our Creator.

Pat Melbourn

El Niño

'If Winter comes, can Spring be far away?' we cry
- each day that passes, Winter slipping by
(at least, that's been the natural way of things
until this crazy, mixed-up Spring of Springs).

Freak floods and snow and icy winds abound
whilst, lured by sun, Spring flowers bloom on the ground
Tornadoes rage and decimate the land
and few of us can really understand
why ice-caps melt, seas rage, and rivers flood
and leave behind their heritage of mud.

In far-off lands, proud forests standing there
still fiercely burn, and smoke fills all the air
and wildlife, trapped by flames (no place to flee)
- cruel hand of nature's misery.

El Niño - caused by warming seas, we've learned
is earth's foundation's legacy returned!

Joyce Newlin

PICTURES FROM THE NATIVITY

Bright and clear shines the star in the heavens,
Illuminating the frozen ground,
Throwing into light relief,
A stable on the edge of town
. . . apparently of little worth,
But chosen for the Saviour's birth.

Joseph the carpenter stands in its doorway,
Contemplating the shining star,
Remembering his vivid dream,
His pregnant wife, their journey far;
Understanding but in part,
Yet trusting God within his heart.

Mary the virgin, her labour over,
Cradles in her arms, her son,
Sleepy, just like other babes,
But to her, the special one -
Jesus Christ, whose destiny,
Beginning now, will set us free . . .

Sheila Burnett

The Cross

Our Lord to a cross they nailed,
He who once they a Saviour hailed,
Thorned crown adorned His brow,
In mocking derision the knee they bow,
His head hung low upon His chest,
Below the crowd mock, jeer and jest,
Rivulets of blood His face ran down,
His brow pierced by thorned crown,
Nails through His hands and feet were driven,
He who for peace and love had striven,
His aching back scarred by steel-tipped lash,
His precious blood upon the crowd did splash,
Despite His suffering and His pain,
Words of reproach He did disdain,
His mother, gentle Mary, gazed upon His face,
Wracked with pain, yet filled with grace,
When another sufferer to Our Lord did call,
He was promised to dwell forever in Heaven's Hall,
From Our Lord's lips there came a groan,
He felt abandoned, on His own,
Yet to His Father to forgive them, He cried,
Then the Prince of Peace, He died,
He who once they a Saviour hailed,
Our Lord to a cross they nailed.

Joe De La Mare

Your Will

I know I'm 'born again', Lord,
My whole life turned around,
My past sin all forgiven,
This lost sheep has been found.
I just need to know your will.

I have this problem now, Lord,
I need to sort it out,
You see, I'm only human
And I want to scream and shout,
'How will I know your will?'

The things I want to do, Lord,
Come readily to hand.
Then off I go, regardless of what
You might, for me, have planned.
Where do I find your will?

Do I find it in your word, Lord,
When I listen with my heart?
Could the preacher hit me with it?
Oh, I don't know where to start!
When will I hear your will?

I really should calm down, Lord,
And trust in what you say.
I have eternal life now and
You're with me all the way.
How blessed is your will.

So I'm praying really hard, Lord,
For your spirit's guiding love
To lead me gently on until
I reach my home above.
Then I shall know your will.

Jay

On Turning A Blind Eye

'We who are strong ought to bear with the failings of the weak and not to please ourselves. Each of us should please his neighbour for his good to build him up' Romans 15:1 & 2

Do we turn a blind eye to our own and other's sin?
Are we blind and deaf because of the world's din?
Are our hearts hard, and our tongues still,
because the cry of sin is so shrill?
Do we turn away when we see pain?
Are we anxious about our own gain?
Do our brothers and sisters have a place in our heart -
or would we rather be apart?
Are we so trapped in our own little world,
that we fail to see the enemy's plan unfurled -
in all its depravity - before our very eyes,
because Satan is a master of disguise.
He will lure, and tempt, and kill, and steal -
but what he offers is not real -
it's meant to harm, to take us to hell,
while he whispers in our ear: 'All is well!'
But don't believe him - he's the Father of Lies -
he will laugh and cheer as this world dies.
He's the plunderer of souls, a murderer, a thief -
the snake lying in wait under every green leaf.
So if he strikes at our friends and does them harm,
as he beguiles and entreats them with all his false charm,
will we be ready to run to them, offer them aid -
or will our weakness and apathy cause our delay,
while our brother or sister lies in the dust of death,
struggling, struggling, to catch their last breath.
And what about us, if *we're* drowning in sin,
would we want someone to rescue us, help pull us in?
Or would we let our pride stifle our yell,
as we slowly and silently slid towards hell,
caught up in the current of sin and shame -
endlessly looking around for someone to blame.

So let us open our eyes to each other's needs.
Let us put God's love into actions and deeds.
That's the way we should be to bring pleasure to God,
we *have* to learn to walk the way Jesus trod.
To bear each other's burdens, with all their pain -
their sickness, their guilt, their sorrow, their shame -
it's the way of the cross, of dying to self -
the way to forgiveness, to wholeness, to health.
it's the only way our lives will reflect God's glory
it's the only way this world will believe our story.

Eunice Harding

THE SPUR OF LIBERTY

Seeking higher bliss, bears curious restlessness,
From state to state, bewildered into fate.

Build a house to suffice old age, sold before the roof is laid.
Sow the flowering garden seeds, rent nearing the bearing trees.

Clear a field for keep, relinquish for others to reap.
Take up a calling, depart the next morning.

Settle in one place, then soon go off in chase.
If granted relaxation, plunge into expedition.

At the close of the day, the ultimate pursuit inevitably,
Precludes before grown tired, hence felicity so vitally desired.

Brandan Friel

JESUS, MY SAVIOUR

Perfect pocket of light above me,
Holding my magnet, my positive ion:
My core and my king - my reason for being,
Enveloped by light.
O source of fervour, of faith and grace;
My crown of creation and star of the heavens.
I am a shadow of you, a dim reflection,
Incompletion without your completeness.
I hunger for you, my vision and thought;
Map of my future, Lord of my heart.
In your hand sits my hope and it radiates warmth;
My palm presses in.
My confidant, confidence and concrete hope
Whose powerful heart beats for me;
Submerge my soul in streams of light as I reach for you,
Piercing the clouds of heaven.
My way, my truth, my life and my freedom,
My iris, my yolk, my centre of all;
I am your prism, your poem, your work in production.
My heart is your home.
Liberate this latent longing within me;
Fill me and finish me, this clay in your hands.
My redemption, release, my peace and my key,
My focus and light, I live only for you.

Jessica Bomford

OUT OF DARKNESS INTO LIGHT

I, now, am a 'child of the light',
Entering gladly into the 'fight'
To banish gloom and sadness here,
No longer walking in darkness and fear.

Shouldering burdens He lovingly prepared,
Unable to carry them without He shared,
Knowing His power is greater than mine,
Casting them all on His love Divine.

Proving Him and His promises true,
Coloured by His rainbow hue.
Strengthened and kept by the 'Light of the world' -
Jesus - my Saviour is *love* unfurled.

Granting me peace as the moments flow,
Healing my body with such a glow
Of Holy Spirit energy - free for all;
Won't *you* hear His redeeming call?

Won't *you* acknowledge your desperate need?
And into your heart let Him plant a seed
Of love and salvation - so freely given
To passport and transport you safe into Heaven.

And to you shall be given eternal riches of grace,
Boundless and pure beyond all trace;
From Jesus who calls unto *you* today,
'I've come to bring Light into your life to stay.'

Edith Ditchburn

Comfort In Bereavement

I lost a loved one yesterday
and life seems lonely and full of despair.
How can I face today
with sad reminders everywhere?

I awake as the dawn begins
with the sky streaked with golden light.
It really does not seem fair
that the day should be so bright.

The morning clouds form patterns
that resemble a shining stair
and then I realise I am not alone
that God is showing me he is there.

My friend has climbed those golden steps
and for me the path ahead
will not always be strewn with sadness
but with happy memories instead.

E Brace

DEATH AND REBIRTH

Death

I am not a poet, and boy! don't I know it.
For if I played that part, I'd have romance in my heart.

What happens when love dies, and I see before my eyes
the former desire of my heart that no longer fits the part?

Is it really all my fault? Should I still my God exalt?
And should I, my faults confessing, sit down and count my blessings?

Or is the cause in another's heart? Does their love no longer play
                                                                               its part?
Has criticism caused my love to die? Did I really make a try?

I really need to know the reason, I can't stand this even for a season.
If not, something's really got to give. I can't say this is how I want
                                                                                   to live.

How do we go about rebirth, bring back some of life's spark and mirth?
Invite the Lord Jesus into the scene; and love can return to where it
                                                                              has been.

This doesn't happen instantly; the hurt is deep though you can't see,
But from the death new love can rise and next time we'll be more wise.

So as I sit in my despair and weep my tears and tear my hair,
I hand it to the Lord in faith and put our lives into His grace.

Rebirth

We've asked God into our lives to sort the problem out
We've put it all in His hands and trust He'll work it out.

Relationships are changing between us you can tell.
We've love and understanding - we used to fight like hell.

It really is amazing the things that God can do.
He alters hate to loving and makes us seem like new.

Joy really comes from living with Jesus in my life:
It has made me more at peace with self and with my wife.

These gifts are freely given: it's not that we deserve;
We're asked to follow daily and both believe and serve.

We can never hope to earn the love God shows to each,
Remember God in daily life and, by example, teach.

We asked for help: He gave it - and not just mild relief.
God's power of re-creation is beyond our best belief.

We lay down our lives in thanks for peace that God has given;
It comes from being open and not from having striven.

That our lives are lived for God is all He ever asks;
And being loved and loving are now our daily tasks.

May our love be everlasting, like the love that God gives,
And may we always share it as long as each one lives.

We praise You God our Father, and praise To Jesus, Son.
We praise You Holy Spirit, Your love has made us one!

Tony Cashmore

HEAR THIS MY PEOPLE ISRAEL

O holy one of the living God who didst walk this land in ages past.
Youth awakened to His eternal call in Temple Courts He sat,
                                                                Israel's will.

Those fine dark eyes of the beardless lad did listened to those sages old words astounding flowed through lips so profounding, iron sharpened iron until that day prepared when youthful form grew; the chosen, he to crush that serpent's head.

Stepped out of Jordan's deep to received the spirit meek and swept into deserts heat to be still for His Father's will.

Robed in peace with kingdom light healed the sick and restored
                                                                      the sight.

Silence was his messianic call yet a lighted beacon, to the blind. Wisdom personified, shone humble virtue.

Disciples drawn from lower mould taught and trained in the master's fold for that great day when tongues of fire would rest so invest this church of ours.

Scribe, Pharisee, Sadducee, clothed in vestments white from these vessels pure and white pour fort scorn on one so rare as grace -
in haste and fury they stole the love so rare with craftiness and cunning as farce proclaimed king he was nailed bare hung there on that tree of wrath, perfect innocence, paid that price so high for me, so too that grace I may receive.

From temple mount on high white smoke lifted to the sky as Levite choirs chant the beginning of that Pascal day. As dusk drew on ten thousand lambs were slain yet did they know not where that true lamb was lain?

That dark hour passed, the deed was done, the Devil thought the victory won. The gentle women bound the body pure with oil and spice all smelling nice and laid him in the tomb.

The heavens declare this mighty act the word had been spoken and became a fact.

While angels sang praises most high the son hears the Father's cry arise! arise! O faithful one, you have proved to be my true beloved son. What joy and hope we can now all rejoice because Jesus sits at the Father's side preparing to meet the new bride. My Lord I know that day is near.

Chris Esom

O DOVE OF PEACE

O dove of peace
grant me wings to fly
allow my pain to cease
and release me to the sky

O dove of joy
wipe away my tears
give me hope in all my years
and punish all my enemies' sneers

O dove of hope
fill me with Christ's realism
His willingness to die for the cause
and His life everlasting

O dove of death
give me eternal life
away from earth
in Christ's countenance and dearth.

Christopher P Gillham

UNTITLED

You are God's creation
Treasured and adored
Whatever others think of you,
You're cherished by the Lord.

A C Edwards

HOW TO COPE WITH THE PROBLEMS IN LIFE

Everyone has some problems in life
We all get our share of strain and strife
They should be accepted without making a fuss
As we all know that Jesus suffered for us
Remember no matter what that problem may be
You do not need to depend on your own strength entirely
To get an answer to a problem of any kind
Faith in Jesus can give you a cure and peace in your mind

Today if you happen to be facing some sorrow
And you feel that you cannot face tomorrow
Do not worry about what lies ahead
Nor about what you shall wear or how you will be fed
Jesus knows your needs and mine
Put your trust in him and all will work out fine
Remember your loved ones are in his care
Whether they are in heaven with him or in the world somewhere

Every day throughout each year
Many people's lives are filled with fear
They have not got the courage to face a task
Nor know that all they have to do is ask
Ask Jesus into their hearts today
To get guidance and help on how to live each day
The problems in life will not all disappear
But with his help there will be nothing to fear

Robert Doherty

My Master's Voice

It came to me.
From whence it came, or why to me?
I know not.
A fleeting breath, a whisper.
As silently as falling leaves
On Autumn breeze . . .
    'Come, follow Me!'

No thunder clap, no ocean roar.
I perceived it dimly
Yet darkness not,
for it pierced my soul
as a shaft of light
within tangible stillness . . .
    'Come, follow Me!'

It came again.
It called my name across the vast expanse
Of time and space.
The unspoken question, 'Me?'
Responded, reverberated.
Yet still it came . . .
    'Come, follow Me!'

Tentatively stepping
through narrow gate, I tread upon
An unknown path.
Decisively. Forsaking all,
I now pursue
that eternal whisper . . .
    'Come, follow Me!'

Stephanie Berry

OMAGH

Omagh paid an awful price
when a bomb went off today
innocents were slaughtered
when evil deceived the way

Young and old from far and near
and the yet unborn
suffered from the madness
that brought a nation's scorn

People in tribute united
for the victims of this crime
a savage senseless act committed
let it be the last and only time

Please God be with them in their suffering
and we pray for their relief
give them inner strength to bear
their broken hearts of grief

They have drained the cup of sorrow and pain
and their lives are now without song
inner strength to look forward
and make them want to live on

Frank Scott

THE EXPLORER

The Explorer clings on frantically to the gnarled and crooked branch
That hangs high above the blazing pit where the flames of
                                                    destruction dance
The branch is cracking and starting to break
As the snake in its leaves is beginning to wake
With no way up and no way down, there's nowhere that he can run
He's managed to find his bullets now, but he forgot to bring his gun

The Explorer hangs on silently, Adventure was his goal
But for the first time now in many long years, he thinks about his soul
If this is the end, then what was it all for?
If it isn't the end, then could there be more?
He was never really bad, but was he that good? He always put himself first
The Explorer's interested in Religion now, the explorer fears the worst

The Explorer looks around him and for the first time slowly sees
The hand of a Creator in nature's skill and ingenuity, in the sun, the sky and trees
In Creation he sees order, Life with Rhythm and Rhyme
Love is the beating heart of it, making it glow and shine
The truth dawns quietly upon him, as he tries to swallow his pride
Love was always there around him, he just never let it get inside

The Explorer clings on frantically to the gnarled and crooked branch
That hangs high above the blazing pit where the flames of destruction dance
Tears sting and burn his eyes with remorse that will not cease
For years he'd roamed and searched the world but never once found peace
Only now he knows and as he dies, he cries to heaven above
I die empty though the world was mine, for I closed my heart to Love

David Overland

BUZZING

Indulge in drink and drugs and sex - then!
Try fill that emptiness inside!
Try dull that hollow feeling;
They don't work. I've tried.

Don't you know you'll never ever get
A bigger or better buzz
From the one in heaven looking down
From the one who made and loves us.

He can fill that need within you
The one you can't quite explain
He can give you love and peace and joy
And take all your hurts and pain.

He can make you smile and laugh without
Even really knowing why!
He's better than any drug I've had
He's now my only high!

Mandy Roberts

CALVARY

Calvary, that blessed spot so dear
Where Jesus bore my sins, my debt to clear
To those scenes my spirit gladly turns
And when I scan that sacrifice my heart doth burn.

From that blest place Thy mercy shown I see
Thy love divine is there made known to me
Boundless grace to all mankind declared
From endless ages by the son of God prepared

Lingering on awhile in meditation sweet
My eyes I rest upon the pierced feet
That bitterest hour my soul doth contemplate
When Jesus bore the brunt of man's hate

Precious thoughts do o'er my spirit roll
They cover all my faults and captivate my soul
Who would not here abide in rapture firm and sweet
While bending low adoring at they feet.

Max Gray

THE HIND OF THE MORNING
(Psalm XXII, 'Aijeleth Shaher', signifies 'The Hind of the Morning'. The great sufferings of Christ, as the hind or hart is in the morning chase; and so hunted down by His enemies until He is surrounded by them (as dogs surround the weary hart) when He hung upon a cross.)

Preceded and ushered in, the darkening shadows gone,
The dew fell on the thirsty ground, earth cried, 'Bring forth the fawn.'
Prepared, as the Morning Star of earth and heaven born,
First rays of Calvary shone afar,
    ('On the hind of the morning.' Dawn.)

He fell! As the dew of heaven, upon a cross forlorn,
To save the fallen sinner, by covenant promise sworn.
The rising sun, a perfect day. The light of heaven adorned,
His going forth prepared the way.
    ('The hind of the morning!' Dawn.)

Comprehend, or count the cost, what knowledge can perform,
God, to redeem the sinner lost, his flesh and blood be torn.
Softly tread this sacred ground, you tread upon a thorn.
Take off your shoes, 'tis holy ground.
    ('The hind of the morning!' Dawn.)

Kept faithful with a single aim,
Although reviled in scorn,
There on the cross they wrote the name,
    ('The hind of the morning!' Dawn.)

Who is he? Called by grace
And not his sin to scorn,
Can look upon the Saviour's face,
    ('The hind of the morning!' Dawn.)

Rich and poor, both low and high, each to his stable born,
Likewise the fool, all wise men die, and still the Saviour scorn,
Yet there was one, I do accord, redemption's blood adorned.
'Remember me, O Lord,' he cried, 'answer for me',
    ('Thou hind of the morning!' Dawn.)

There all heaven kept the night
O'er the hind of the morning long,
To meet the first opening morning light,
Earth's watchman cried,
    'The Dawn'

T C Adams

SILENT PRAYER

Lift me
slow like a sunrise

Carry me
through the stone dyke passage
and prickly nettle moat
where ferns bend low
with archangel wings
and bright-eyed forget-me-nots
bow at your feet.

Take me higher
than a lapwing's dream
to where love speaks
silent, deep and green
when words matter not
in the
company of trees.

Kathy Stewart

THE GIFT OF LIFE

Life is such a wonderful gift
a gift that is true and complete.

It is a gift accepted and loved by husband and wife on the day of birth,
It is a gift that causes pain and anxiety to the unmarried mother.
It is a gift destroyed by the oppressor, the powerful.

It is a gift that was nailed to a tree
because the world could not accept the gift,
It is a gift that shattered the tomb
because some cherished the gift.

It is a gift we celebrate at the dawning of the day.
It is a gift we give thanks for at the end of the day.

It is a gift that is seen in
the unseeing eyes of the blind.
It is a gift that is lived in,
the broken bodies of the sick, the lame.

It is a gift of uncertainty to the young
unemployed and fearful,
It is a gift of burden to the old,
ignored and forgotten.

It is a gift that reaches out to us
from the undernourished body of the starving child,
It is a gift that speaks to us
from the streets of Soweto, Belfast, Gaza.

Yes, life is a wonderful gift,
I pray that we will protect it!

Andrew Lawler

THE FEAST

Lord, to your table we are led,
Remembering your broken body and the blood you shed,
We come as we are, we need our spirits fed,
You, Lord, are the Bread of Life,
So feed us with that Bread.

We need to drink of you Lord,
As you drank the cup,
So quench our thirsting souls, Lord,
and fill us up.
We come to meet you here, O Living word.
In the quiet and stillness, may your voice be heard,
So as together we partake of this Bread and Wine,
Fill us Holy spirit with Love Divine.

Betty Jones

A Troubled Friend

As my heart is joined to yours in this journey home to Heaven;
I can't not feel you're pain, so these words to you I'm given.

I see us all as seeds planted on earth to be sown;
You're seed has been nurtured since childhood by you're Mum and
now it's grown.

By your own will you accepted God as you're gardener to watch over
you're roots;
And He has been doing so, for I can see you're shoots.

I think to myself 'What kind of flower is God making you to be;
Only He knows what kind, is it a lily, a tulip, a daisy or is it a
giant tree?'

The weather hasn't been good to you're stems these past days. But God
is all good and as a gardener, he's the best;
He's pruning you friend, it's hard work and the gardener has to rest.

But He's still watching over His prize flower and waiting for the sun to
come out;
And when you feel the sun warming you're buds and making you smile,
You'll know what all the pain was all about.

For it's then you will bloom and be God's delight and joy;
Then He will pluck you up and take you home to His garden in heaven.
Oh boy!

I imagine myself to be some day, a daffodil and to be planted next to
you in His garden so sweet;
So rejoice and be glad as we are being pruned and in heaven we
will surely meet.

Anne McLeod

FOR MY PARENTS AND MY CHILDREN

I came here to help you,
You were stuck you see.
You called out to God for help,
God sent me.
Pretend to be a child he said,
Some souls are lost in pain.
Help them to remember,
The reason why they came.

So I was born to you a son,
I came to set you free.
I gave the only gifts a child could give,
To help you see.
But you couldn't heed my message,
You couldn't understand.
You thought that I was just a child,
Dismissed me out of hand.

I came to say don't live like this,
Don't die like this I say.
I'll show you how to wear your love,
So you can find your way.
But in this place, of fear and anger,
A victim I became.
And all my good intentions,
We're gone like summer rain.

So now I call out to God,
Send me someone too.
And God in perfect wisdom,
Knew to send me you.

Phil Millichip

THE NIGHT OUR HOPE WAS BORN

The moon rose over Bethlehem
On that night long ago.
The mystery that the night would bring,
Those shepherds weren't to know
When that little Infant King was born
In a stable cold and bare
To die triumphant on a cross
And make us all his heir.

The angels sang their song of joy
And led the shepherds to the boy
The star appeared so clear and bright
And brought the Wise Men to this sight
God's greatest gift, His only Son
The King of Kings, the Holy One
What was ahead they did not know
That night in Bethlehem long ago.

Although we killed him on that cross
Who came to save us from all loss
He still pleads for us on High
As His return is drawing nigh,
'Great Father, may they know your love
And every blessing from above
Grant them knowledge so they know
I came to Bethlehem long ago.

Alwyn Wilson

UNTITLED

Quietly falls the night -
one by one the petals
of our day float down.
The flower's heart is left
and the seeds of tomorrow.
Peace! For the day is done.
Joy! For tomorrow comes.
Sleep, deeply sleep
At rest in God.

Isobel Howden

At A Winter Dawn

And I have been,
and I have been
at intersections of your love
with energy as matter seen
around, within, above.

O make me now,
O make me now
your living particle of will
to grow in power and allow
me your time to fulfil.

O may I seek,
O may I seek
the heartbeat of your mystery
in things that, in appearance weak,
become your power free.

Then show me Lord,
then show me Lord
the path to see my real self
beyond the poverty of word
in silence's true wealth.

So shall I be,
so shall I be
incarnate with your spirit, grow
to wave-crest on your living sea,
and time's frail secret know.

John Barnes

HANDS

Whose hands grabbed you in the garden
Dragging you to trial?
Whose hands struck the glancing blows
Causing you to stumble?
Whose hands wielded the whip
While Pilate washed his?
Whose hands poured the water
That he thought would cleanse him of your blood?
Whose hands ripped your clothing?
Offered you wine mixed with drugs?
Placed the cross on bloody shoulders
Skin shredded from cruel lashes?
Whose hands pushed, pulled and whipped you
On the road to Golgotha?
Whose hands flung you to the ground
Across the rough wood?
Stretched your arms, wrenching them apart,
Not knowing that you would thus embrace the world?
Whose hands took that hammer and those nails,
Driving them through sacred flesh
Ripping, tearing, grating?
Whose hands lifted the crossbeam
Bringing it down with a jolt that tore through your body?
Whose hands offered you vinegar and water?
Wielded the spear that pierced your side?
And after you committed yourself into the hands of your father,
Whose hands took you down from the cross?
Carried you mournfully away?
Wrapped your body?
Placed you lovingly in the tomb?

Sue Fenton

PILGRIMAGE

Build a cairn of faithfulness out of the steep ascent,
Absorb, in a breath of solitude, the struggle of deep intent.
Release the rough-hewn anguish, embedded hurt or sin
To shape the cornerstone of love, God's Spirit lies within.

Let each stone of remembrance sanctify the whole,
Integrate experience, liberate the soul.
Where through perseverance, the best becomes the least,
Memorial of humbleness, gift in kind grant peace.

Altar, as a landmark of a life expressed,
Pathway straight and narrow or uncertain, rugged quest.
Fashion each memorial that trust and truth uphold.
Find through love that suffers, patience self-control.

Look out into the distance from summit, mountain peak.
Let the glorious overview of God's intention speak.
In offering the fragment, the disparate journey's tread.
Let the solace of the Spirit renew the covenant made.

In the steps that falter on the downward way,
May the heart find courage, to face another day.
For the cairn stands witness, for the world to see
That life in Spirit faith resolved, holds integrity.

Judith A Pye

OPEN VERDICT

There is a wind
That weeps upon the sand.
There are thoughts
Words cannot understand.
There are moments
Time cannot count,
Wonders none will surmount.
And where were we
When they were writing history?
Not knowing defeat
Or finding victory,
Or caring much for
All their idiocy.

Vera Boyle

SPRING (OR RESURRECTION)

In the wild wind's teeth we watched and waited,
Hostage held, remote and isolated
From all life and growing thing,
Longing, yearning for the spring.

Life lies buried in deep obscurity:
Concealed, unborn, in pristine purity.
Graciously waits in innocence,
To burst forth in omnipotence!

God's green garden gives again its grace -
Splendour and colour and freshness of face.
Spring's strength o'ercomes: life has burst!
Winter's bitter blasts dispersed!

Life leaps out from death's dark silence,
Glorious in magniloquence!
Put away all introspection -
Witness this great resurrection!

Jean Wilford Hodgson

INSECTS

Come, Belinda, sit with me,
Look at ant and louse and bee,

See their legs,
And watch their wings,

And then, my dearest, youngest daughter,
You'll learn to love, and not to slaughter.

Irene Tester

HOLY INNOCENTS' DAY

In Ramah now no tears are shed;
no distraught mother's keening cry
to mourn the hallowed infant dead;
of life bereft, by reason lost
The life by writ of Heaven decreed
now riven from the entrusted host;
This Holy gift, this precious seed
despised by one it trusted most.
No mother's love to hold and cherish.
'The choice is mine, the child must perish!'

No mother's love to hear the cry.
No weeping voices heard in Ramah;
a cold steel probe to pierce and pry;
A silent scream unheard on Earth
across the raging vaults of Heaven echoes,
Mama!
Why?

And Heaven looks on in anguished disbelief;
while we on earth who stifle grief
nor yet cry out - must share the soul-destroying shame
and with the unnatural mother bear the blame
and Jesus from the cross cries out -
Father in Heaven, forgive, forgive!
I die that these who kill might live.

Derek N Thorp

St Olaf's, Wasdale Head

The church is just another
small stone barn, slate-roofed.
Around it a group
of ancient yews
huddles for comfort.
Upon the valley
the burden of the mountains
lies heavy.

We limp through the door
crippled with fear,
kneel in a cramped pew
beside a low window
through which this same landscape
asserts its presence.

Has God, too, sought
the shelter of this building,
this inclement morning,
driven down from the high peaks,
the snow-sifted ridges,
to visit briefly
this yearning altar?

The longer we absorb
the utter silence, the harder
it becomes to say which
is the greater intensity of longing,
His or ours.

Monica Ditmas

Was It For Me, Lord?

Was it for me, Lord?
The crown of thorns, the scourge, the cross?
Can I believe such love that bore so much - for me?
That very God, from heaven's glory
Should descend to earth, to pain, to death
Because of love?
    I must believe, or else such sacrifice would be in vain.
    I do believe, my Lord, and am raised up
    In worship and in love -
    A pale reflection of thine own,
    But mine to offer through thy Spirit's gift alone.

Stella Morton

CHRISTMAS DAY

Is there joy at heaven's gate,
And will the world from sleep awake,
To greet upon this spacious morn
The Holy Child of Mary born?

In truth the heavenly gates resound,
Where all celestial songs abound,
And global psalms shall never tire,
Awake is earth! This myriad choir.

And earthly bells tell out their tale,
Their *Christus Rex* runs through the vale,
And sleepy towns and children stir,
By mistletoe and prickly fir.

And there amid the sparkling trees
The waiting church - the surpliced parson on his knees
While carols swing full-down the nave
To rise above its rich arcade.

And festive-trimmed the high street inn,
Where old men swear about the jukebox din,
And the barmaid with peroxide hair
Just chews her gum with an indifferent stare.

And think of those who belted-up the tried M1
To beat the breathalyser they passed The Rising Sun
And all those children who enjoy computer games,
When most of us are over-fed and suffer stomach pains.

Yet in the trailing Glastonbury Thorn,
I see the cruel Crown of Thorns,
And in black-boughed holly berries red -
The Blood of Christ in wine and bread.

Derek Marshall

SORROW

Unquiet grave for living men
Is the soul's torment when
Parting grows to separation.
Leaves fall and grasses flatten:
Life ebbs to a new pattern.
Dolorous change makes sad dreams,
And tired hearts lack means
To make music.
Only the sounds of death's lament
Fall by the lonely tent
Where sorrow dwells:
And people pass like strangers
Wearing veils.

There was one born in a manger
Who walked this road
And faced this danger:
Whom death could not hold,
And is no stranger
To those who mourn.

Emrys George

REASSURANCE

When all seems dark and hopeless
And life is full of woe,
Recall the softness of a kitten's fur
And the warmth of a sunset's glow.

And marvel at an opening flower,
The joy of a blackbird's call -
The delight on the face of a tiny child
Who'll soon be strong and tall.

Then hear the sound of laughter,
Of music clear and sweet
As happy feet go dancing
To that strong, hypnotic beat.

So when there's sadness in your world
And all seems black and drear,
Look for God in small things
And know that He is here.

Eileen M Pratt

BEFORE YOU GET ANGRY
(A poem for me)

Before you get angry
Be sure that your brother was wrong.
Think of the shame and the pain
Think of the gulf, the ache, the void,
- Could it be that you are mistaken? -
Think of the hard, steep, stubborn steps,
Cutting, one by one, in cold, resistant rock
You will have to climb -
Both have to climb -
To reach that sheer gold summit again
Where on that blue and sunlit day
The view for two was so wonderful.

Why is it that that Fool Pride
Insists one can never be wrong?
Down on one's knees is better
Scrubbing a floor
Or to chant the magnifcat in a chapel
Or mud-dabble in a garden
To plant the tiniest seeds that grow
To spread into a mustard tree
Which may provide a higher perspective.

I wonder if the smallest animals -
Ants, beetles, flies, grasshoppers, caterpillars
Really have a safer, sounder world view?
As far as I know
I've never been an ant, beetle, fly, grasshopper or caterpillar,
But when I get angry with a friend or brother
How I sometimes wish I were!

E Gwen Gardner

FRIENDS' MEETING

Slow the heart. Clear the head.
Walk silent to the meeting place
Expectantly, no holy dread,
No guarantee, just hope for grace.

Sit silent with the other Friends
To hear the word the spirit sends
And hope I won't get up to speak,
Renouncing all that's to the meek.

But if I'm called then rise I must;
That is the due I have to pay.
Though I be neither good nor just
I walk with God the narrow way.

Walter Birmingham

OUR LADY'S STATUE

I have a tiny statue, about two inches high:
An image of Our Lady, and one I didn't buy.

I won it from a cracker, one Christmas now long gone.
The crackers were called 'Holy', manufactured in Taiwan.

My statue's made of plastic. It's hollow up inside.
Our Lady stands quite upright, with arms extended wide.

I hardly dare admit it - it makes me wince to tell -
This gruesome little likeness is luminous as well!

You cannot see the features (too small to have a face).
Despite it being so tacky, it still holds pride of place.

I keep it in the kitchen, behind the kitchen sink.
It only has the merit of causing me to think.

I think about Our Lady. Her memory lends a spark
To all my common housework, and twinkles in the dark!

I don't subscribe to cheapness; I don't approve of 'grot',
But when it comes to praying, *that's* what my statue's got.

This tiny little tribute to all the worst in art
Promotes the finest homage to Our Lady, from my heart.

Penny Fenn Clark

The Poet Momentarily Sees His Surroundings Transformed

('The world was made flesh and dwelt among us, and we beheld his beauty.')

    He saw the heavenly moment come
    Unheralded, unmarked, unsung.
    He watched the magic slowly pass.
    The frost still stood upon the grass,
    The sun crept up the rising day
    And swept the miracle away;
    Yet all was changed, - the world was new.
    The poet felt what he must do:
'Each time that God is fleshed,' said he,
'Someone must sing a litany.
I am the angel choir that sings;
The shepherds and the three wise kings.
No gold, incense or myrrh I bring
But this is all my offering: -
To tell the unbelieving Earth
That God himself is come to birth
Here in this world of you and me
For those that have the eyes to see;
Again conceived, and yet again,
The seed of God, the holy grain,
The inward light, eternal word.
My soul doth magnify the Lord,
For I am Mary, too and see
The Spirit brooding over me.
Here, in my inmost part, I know
A spiritual embryo.'

'I sing that you, and you, and you
May seek and know the infant too;
'Magnificat' together cry,
My soul the Lord doth magnify.'

R E Hope-Simpson

HOLD ME

Always drifting from here to there
Never will my mind stand still
Being everywhere and nowhere
That's my dharma to fulfil

Ancient wisdom of moon and sun
The religions of the East
Jesus Christ - where have you gone
What's the number of the beast

Philosophy and biology
Brought together with twenty-three
Different points of view for me
Yet I don't know how to be free

On my shoulders - it lays hard
The heavy burden of emptiness
And it takes me further apart
Whereto - I cannot even guess

Hold me
But not too tight
Let me be free
And lead me through the night.

Charlie Blackfield

THE MORROW'S DAWN

'Oh what am I, that I should stay,
when others have long left the fray?
With cannon wrecked and bowmen fled,
and swordsmens' blood o're this field is shed!

Oh what am I, in this my plight,
that I should dally till the light?
To meet the foe on morrow's dawn,
with my army gone, and all forlorn,

Oh who am I, that I should take
upon my shoulders every stake?
For am I not as every man
that's borne arms for this clan?

Oh what am I, but flesh and blood
when the storm has reached the flood?
For my bones cannot dispel
those fires of the Devil's Hell!

Oh Master, why can I not flee
as others have this night, left me?
For with good reason I have known
I shall only reap, what I have sown.'

D J Cleeves Snr

MURDER AT THE DAMASCUS GATE

How could I do it?
Just stand there watching coolly,
as blood trickled down
first from one cheek, then the other,
then from his forehead, until he crumpled
in a heap, under a heap of rocks,
and not in a shamed, hidden place
but against the city wall, where all could see.

Of course, I didn't actually do a thing,
- just stood there holding a coat.
It wouldn't have been right to sully my hands
with a sinner's blood,
I, who was brought up to be pure
 - to hate the sinner and the heretic.
But I had to be there, to see, to make sure he died,
like the one he said he followed,
 - the one he said he loved.

Love!
They didn't teach us that at school,
except to love God - not a man who dies.
So what on earth was he about?

Only my mother loved in that way,
a poor sickly child like me.
She was patient and kind,
never wanted what others had,
Never boasted to the neighbours.
or complained about their kids.
She never reminded me of all the things,
that I did wrong,
Nor gossiped about what others got up to.

She just went on loving them,
whatever they were like.
And it never got her anywhere.
So that's why I stood there,
Keeping myself pure at the city gate,
Before going for that top job in Damascus.

Tony Latham

WHY?
(Translation of Eden Asem Aba Na by Ko Nimo)

The Irish boys had come to us in March.
Good Catholic homes. Shining buds of men.
Ours had loved them, speaking without language.
We prepared ours for the return visit:
Clothes, tickets, passports, gifts for their hosts,
Yet unseen, save on rectangles of Kodak paper.

We drove them to Santander in the August heat.
Newest growth on our families' trees.
Waved 'Vaya con Dios,' trying to still
Our heart pinches with their excitement.
Celts all; how could anything go wrong?
By phone we heard of their safe arrival.

Their first holiday beyond our Spanish shores.
They saw their school, went to Mass at their church.
Cusp of the trip a journey further north.
What is a Folk Festival? We found the town on the map.
Twenty-eight went up that day. Two were ours.
Omagh means something different now.

Shirley Cowling

ARE YOU A CHRISTIAN?

'Words strain, crack, and sometimes break.'
No words of ours can ever make
A lasting statement we can take as touchstone for the test.
Perhaps the Word that John perceived, the light unquenched all men received
And still receive, if but believed, dispenses with the rest.
But men seek more. Each from his viewpoint make his 'model', partly true,
Which lasts a while and gives a clue (no model is the best).

So, if your model sets the frame for actions fired by the flame
Which burns in Christ, can you not claim to be a Christian?
And maybe use the thought-forms of your day and man's new-found self-knowledge in a way
That leads to growth and let them say: 'Your way's not Christian!'
For ancient modes (though dearly bought!) can't serve as vehicles for our thought.

We worship that free will be brought to answer God's behest,
An aspiration other faiths proclaim in different metaphor. So if their flame
Described in our own terms, is yet the same as Christ's, pass they the test?
No matter! Let words servants be, not masters, that we might agree
In all our diverse ways to see God's world as one community,
Wherein the sacred mystery that lies beyond all thought can be
Made known within our hearts and free to touch us wordlessly.

David Senior

THE BIBLE

Many words
the Bible holds,
Psalms and Proverbs
Parables . . .
Two Testaments
old and new
tells of folk
like me and you . . .
The Rich and Poor
the good and bad,
The Crucifixion
of our Lord!

A simple book
austere maybe
to stubborn minds
who just won't see
the Truth in each
and every page . . .
How we can profit
if we Believe . . .

Christ gave His life
that we find Love . . .
And find the True Path
Back to God.

Mary Skelton

SEEDS

Umbrellas, wings and plumes,
Like His love, flung out upon the world
By a profligate Creator.
From pods and pepper pots they come,
Twirling, whirling, exploding,
Drifting, falling.
Cups and shells lie shattered
As the heavy weights drop.
A cloud of willowherb
Holds dew's diamonds.
Sparkling spectrums, glow-worms,
Gone in a puff of wind.
Such extravagance, superabundance,
Life and death,
Hoping for resurrection.

Elizabeth Rumsey

THE FACE OF CHRIST

His is the face of every man,
Reflecting the joy, the fear, the pain,
The pity, the anguish, the sorrow we bear,
The life of humanity, he came to share.

His is the face, no man can portray;
His inward peace, all men enfolding,
His bond with Mankind and God above,
No man could paint the face of Love

Winnie Oakley

SNAPSHOTS

In warm, wartime sunshine a bronzed baby lies
On a rug on a lawn; her laughing dark eyes
Look up at me now from the flat album page.
Is it me that I see in that long-ago age?

An old bath, my ocean, a garden my shore,
My ship's safe in harbour, far-off from the war.
Cocooned in my ignorance, boldly I stare,
My boots at half-mast and a bow in my hair.

I pose on a breakwater, already six,
In wrinkle-ruched swimsuit, my legs like two sticks.
No beach babe in embryo, just skin and bone;
No calories to count and no muscles to tone.

Here's me with my mother, there's me with my dad.
I'll never deserve all the love that I had.
I carelessly took all that they had to give;
They taught me to play, and to pray, and to live.

They said I was special - a chosen child; I
Was uncomprehending, I never asked why.
Was it just chance or perhaps God's special plan
Brought me to this woman, brought me to this man?

The years flicker faster as each leaf is turned.
There's no turning back now, my bridges are burned.
Those black and white snaps a charmed childhood portray;
What rainbows remembered through spectrums of grey!

Wendy Mead

WHO NEEDS A TELEPHONE?

I was tempted by the devil
And I gave my Lord a ring
I didn't use a telephone
But he heard everything
I told him of my troubles
How temptation came my way
He guided me to righteousness
Along the straight highway
So whenever I'm in trouble
I give my Lord a call
Then I'm on the straight and narrow
He makes sure I never fall
So if you're tempted by the devil
And he whispers in your ear
Just call the Lord and listen in
You'll have nothing more to fear
Just call him up at any time
But don't get too enraged
There's one thing that you'll never find
That he's otherwise engaged

Euphemia McKillop

A Future

I dream of a day, when the 'Calls to Arms' all die
and the children of this world no longer have to cry
of a day when we can see, our faults, before another's
and we live in peace together as sisters and brothers.
Of a day when we can hope for a future full of love
with a King in whom we trust, who will come from up above
of a day when we can say, 'Love is all around'
When our Lord lives among us and is finally crowned

Vernon Breese

LOVE

I sit at your feet,
Leaning against your knee.
Your hand on my shoulder,
Your breath on my hair.
So close, so intimate -
Can this be real?
I can't believe I'm here, now
Reaching out and touching you.
Two hearts, one soul.
You call my name
with infinite love and gentleness.
I respond joyfully and give You
My heart, my life, my all.

Elizabeth Lang

HE HAS RISEN

Nails and Cross and empty tomb,
Symbols of our Saviour's power.
Satan conquered, death defied,
In our history's greatest hour.

Not a mighty ruler's son
With much attendant pomp and fuss,
But in a lowly stable born
Of simple parents just like us.

In the temple when a child
Learned sages he amazed
Wisdom far beyond his years
Eloquently he displayed.

Throughout his life he preached the word
Telling how he came to save,
He helped the poor and healed the sick
And called the sleepers from the grave.

Forsaken by his closest friends
Condemned and crucified was he,
But Death's dark powers were overcome
He rose again for you and me.

Janet Cavill

What Is Wrong?

What makes you want to run away?
What has happened to you today?
Remember Satan can destroy
Only your flesh, so there is joy.
Your soul is quite beyond his reach.
Have you the faith the Gospels preach?
To keep Gethsemane in mind
Is good advice for all mankind.
Christ told Peter: 'Thou shalt deny me thrice,
This very night, ere the cock crows twice.'

Joe Latham

Parsifal: Or Good Friday Falls On All Fools' Day

This April is all death,
The most real thing is sin
With wages in advance
And time to spend them in.

The willow tree is angered by the wind,
The church bell blown off-key:
Howling iridescence
And the walk to Calvary.

God is infinitely bored
By this procession
Of seasonal banalities
But he makes no digression.

He cannot do otherwise
For his property is extreme:
To be the bloody eternal God
With a passion to redeem.

Peter Mullen

A New Life

I have been searching
through the realms of dark and light;
I have been searching,
for something,
to make my life seem right.

I have found
the darkness holds loneliness, pain and fear;
I have found,
in the light,
that 'someone' holds me near.

Oh Jesus!
I didn't know you were there.
Oh Jesus!
Your light,
takes away loneliness, pain and fear.

I didn't know,
you have loved me since I was born.
I didn't know,
it was for me,
you were crucified, bruised and torn.

You forgave me,
for all I did in the past.
You forgave me,
and loved me,
made me whole, completed at last.

I'll love you,
until I go to my appointed place.
I'll love you,
dear Lord,
and that day I'll see you, face-to-face.

Norma M Smith

A Note Without A Song

I am a note that pipes in the wind.
    Meaningless while I am free,
Astray from the Song of Creation, sung
    In the Halls of Eternity.
I am a note in search of a song:
    And the Song is in search of me.

Louie Horne

MY LORD

My Lord I prayed -
you answered my prayer
you took my hand
you were there.
I someone who had often said
You did not exist -
But when I was at my
lowest ebb -
I called your name -
you took my hand
pulled me out from a dark
deep pit -
I who had sinned against you -
      You forgave.

Meryl Tookaram

A Christmas Poem

I carved some figures out of clay,
The ox and ass and a few little sheep,
And Joseph and Mary in the hay.
I took them down to the Church
To place in the Christmas crib;
But someone had got there first.

I fashioned a silver star
And the angels with golden wings,
And covered them all with glitter
To hang on the Christmas tree;
But when I arrived at my friend's house
He said he'd no room for my things.

I took up my pen
To write a poem
And thought of all the Christmas things
The manger, the shepherds, the three wise Kings,
But I could not think of anything new.
It had all been said before.

I went to the Church alone
And knelt at the altar rail
And knew as I prayed
That I'd nothing to bring
To the Lord, my King
But myself.

And the angels sang
And the stars shone bright,
And the candle flames
Glowed in the night,
And Christ came down and entered in
And turned my darkness into light.

Beryl Johnson

STREET SONG

As I was walking down World's Main Street,
All sorts and conditions of folk did I meet.
Some worked with brain - some with their hands,
In different places: from different lands.
All tongues and colours, creeds and ideas,
Hopes and ambitions, sorrows and fears
And much I found, made me rejoice,
Contented smile and happy voice.
But I had not been travelling long,
When I heard a discord in the song.
For, with one tune, I heard another,
Beside the pavement was the gutter.
There, I saw the other side,
A hell - on - earth, jaws gaping wide,
Heard refugee's cry - saw starving mother,
And kerbside brawl - brother 'gainst brother.
In contrast to the pavement's gold,
Of high ideals and progress bold,
Was the gutter, filled with filth and slime,
The sludge of lust, oppression, crime.
I shrank away - yet realised,
If I would gain the other side,
Then through the gutter I must pass,
Before I reached my home, at last.
For here, decay, disease, defeat
Is part, with the gold, on World's Main Street.
Then said the God, who was there to begin it,
'This is My World and you are in it.
This is your job. This is your task.
To make it my Heaven . . . is all I ask!'

Ramsay Hall

SINGS OF THE KINGDOM OF GOD

Laughter by the lake
And joy of friendship known.
Seedlings of ideas planted
And well-watered shoot up and grow.

Silence in the chapel and union with God
Psalms of praise and songs of joy
A preacher's enthusiasm inspired by the Spirit
The desire to dwell in the house of the Lord for ever.

An unexpected call from a friend
Sharing ideas and making plans.
A greeting from some dear old folk
A glance from colleague, all will be well.

Death after a long hard struggle
Robbing the dignity and quality from life.
Sorrow felt for friendships' end
And yet a sense of peace descends.

Blazing at the end of another day
A sinking sun, a great ball of fire
A sky full of red and pink and grey,
Signs of the Kingdom, my heart's desire.

Gill Sathyamoorthy

SNAKE IN A TREE

I mistook him this time,

Waiting like a fool on my belly
In a luscious garden. He came
To a town's backyard disguised
With squalor and shame.

You see, I was disadvantaged from the start. I did my worst, of course:

I whispered in a bad king's ear.
I took him to a wilderness, face
To face to disabuse him of true
Notions of his time and place.

I misinformed rulers,
Screamed a crowd's bad breath,
I tortured him, and jeered at him,
I nailed him to his death.

But, as I have said, in all of this I was disadvantaged.

He leapt from the cross
And turned on me
And tossed me into
The boughs of this tree,

A fallen angel
Made radiant for light
Squirming and shining this
Black December night.

The children point,
Faces sparkle with glee
At the coloured lights
Coiled in the tree.

Andrew Moll

MARTYRDOM

Martyrdom is witness
To the whole truth.
Alban, Laurence, Stephen and George
Witnessed in blood by death,
While Patrick, Hilda, Augustine and John
Witnessed by life laid down
In toil, to proclaim the truth.
Yet all of these are martyrs,
Whether by word or deed,
Whether in life or death,
For both sides of the coin show the Face
Of God, Who is the Truth.

Teresa Finlayson

JERUSALEM

The Golden Gate was closed,
Walled-up, and had been so
For many years,
No longer waiting
For the arrival of Messiah
In great triumph
But to a promise linked,
One day to return
In glorious majesty
With praise in song and trumpet.
We entered near the western wall
And watched the prayers.
Then, in the rain,
Barefoot we entered
First Al Aqsa and then
In all its splendour
The Golden Dome.
We touched the rock of sacrifice
And of Mohammed's dream
And of his heavenly visit,
And on our walk
Along the Via Dolorsoa
Experiencing the stations,
We thought of that last journey
And a greater 'taking up',
Ascension to the Life hereafter.

Patrick Barker

LOVE AND FAITH

Do not let your heart be sad or sorrowful on this day,
I will be always close to you, never far away.
What we were to one another, so it will always be
In thought's reflective moments, have faith, you will see.

If we had not known precious moments to treasure,
Against love for each other and self to measure
Love foundations, of rock strength, of its power
Built on faith reaching high, our human heavenly tower.

Love and the holy spirit lives forever on,
Our very essence of who we are, of distant realms beyond,
Of all creation in life we found to share,
I will be ever close to you, still deeply care.

When you gather in the rose droplets of early morning dew,
Look deep within its heart, I am there with you.
How we watched, loved the lambs in flowered meadows green,
I am still with you there, now unseen.

Had we not known love's blessing that it gives,
If I had not known you, how would I have truly lived?
For in God's time he will bring together, born again in love we knew
Now through our Christian faith in the world in which we grew.

Albert King

Untitled

Sparrows, sparrows - many sparrows
On the highway - cars are passing
Some are killed - oh, what a shame
Does anyone care?

People, people - many people
Millions now on this fair earth
Danger threatens - violence; famine; war:
Does anyone care?

Our *Lord* said 'Yes,' because
Not even one sparrow is forgotten by God
And *you* and I are worth much more
Trust God, for He *does* care.

M Petch

INFORMATION

We hope you have enjoyed reading this book - and that you will continue to enjoy it in the coming years.

If you like reading and writing poetry drop us a line, or give us a call, and we'll send you a free information pack.

Write to :-
**Triumph House Information
1-2 Wainman Road
Woodston
Peterborough
PE2 7BU
(01733) 230749**